Praise for *Exactly Where to Start*

"The first step is the hardest but Phil Jones will get you to take a giant leap with this poignantly powerful book."
—**Jay Baer,** hall of fame speaker and *New York Times* bestseller

---

"Phil Jones was put on this planet with an entrepreneurial spirit, laser-sharp mind and a determined work ethic that has yielded incredible individual success. He has earned the industry 'chops' to take any business and set it on a course to thrive. In *Exactly Where to Start* Phil equips you with the mindset you need to achieve and the real action steps you need to take to make your IDEA come to life."
—**Lou Diamond,** CEO of THRIVE and author of *Master the Art of Connecting*

"You want to do your own Great Work: a project with impact, a project with meaning. Of course you feel anxious. Phil Jones shows you how to tip the balance away from the fear and toward the excitement, so you

can step over the threshold and begin. Phil Jones shows you exactly how to start."
—**Michael Bungay Stanier,** author of the *Wall Street Journal* bestseller, *The Coaching Habit*

———————

"For any entrepreneur who wants to move from aspiration to action, this is all you will need to kick start your big idea. Consider it the 'Tao of Possibility'."
—**Leslie Ehm,** founder and chief fire-starter of Combustion Training

———————

"Phil M. Jones has done it again! He's taken a concept that many people overcomplicate and he's made it simple. He's made it practical. He's made it doable. Phil has created a powerful action-packed guide—a play-book if you will—to help you actualize your vision for success. If you're like most people… taking the first step is the scariest and most challenging part of the journey. Thankfully Phil will show you *Exactly Where to Start*!"
—**Alan Stein, Jr.**

———————

"Phil Jones is one of the smartest, most strategic entre-preneurs I've encountered. In *Exactly Where to Start* he

helps you develop the mindset and action plan needed to make your own big idea a reality. It's filled with brilliant insight distilled into easy-to-digest lessons that will work in any field."
—**Trena White,** principal of Page Two Strategies

"Phil M. Jones is a person who takes action. Not just any action, but strategic objective-oriented action; smart action. He moves fast, learns fast, and progresses forward. He dreams, he strategizes, he jumps. As a result, he has built a career unlike the likes that most will ever achieve and, at the time of the writing of this book, he's still years away from his fourth decade on this planet.

How does he do it? By following a precise blueprint that he has developed over time and that lends to his success—and if failure is involved, it lends to quick failure, so he can course-correct and regain traction. Fortunately for the rest of us, he has laid this precise blueprint out within this book.

As with his other two EXACTLY books, *Exactly Where To Start* is a simple yet powerful read. It's designed in a way to give you precisely what you need to get your BIG idea up and running as quickly, as realistically, and as successfully as possible.

If you're serious about taking an idea that excites and ignites you but are unsure as to where to start and how to make it your reality, then read this book and put it into action. Then, share your success with the world—and with Phil. He did, after all, write this book for you!"
—**Melissa Agnes,** Crisis Management Advisor, Keynote Speaker, and Author of *Crisis Ready: Building an Invincible Brand in an Uncertain World*

———————

"The hardest thing for most people is to get started. Once again, Phil Jones delivers a book that is concise and actionable. You get exactly what you need when it comes to knowing exactly how to start. The surprise though is how Phil makes the inside work—the mindsets and overcoming the obstacles that hold us back, equally actionable. The perfect little book to get your big idea going!"
—**Jeffrey Shaw,** brand consultant, host of Creative Warriors podcast, and author of *LINGO: Discover Your Ideal Customer's Secret Language and Make Your Business Irresistible*

EXACTLY
WHERE
TO START

EXACTLY

Phil M. Jones

The Practical Guide
to Turn Your BIG
Idea into Reality

WHERE
TO START

WILEY

Cover design: Wiley

Copyright © 2018 by John Wiley & Sons, Inc. All rights reserved.

Published by John Wiley & Sons, Inc., Hoboken, New Jersey.

Published simultaneously in Canada.

For general information on our other products and services or for technical support, please contact our Customer Care Department within the United States at (800) 762–2974, outside the United States at (317) 572–3993 or fax (317) 572–4002.

Wiley publishes in a variety of print and electronic formats and by print-on-demand. Some material included with standard print versions of this book may not be included in e-books or in print-on-demand. If this book refers to media such as a CD or DVD that is not included in the version you purchased, you may download this material at http://booksupport.wiley.com. For more information about Wiley products, visit www.wiley.com.

Library of Congress Cataloging-in-Publication Data has been applied for and is on file with the Library of Congress.

ISBN 9781119484622 (Hardcover)
ISBN 9781119484660 (ePDF)
ISBN 9781119484684 (ePub)

Printed in the United States of America.

V10003383_081618

For Iris – My first mentor

Contents

The Secret Handshake of the Self-Made Man

In my circles, when people think of someone as being "self-made" there is a strong possibility they reference me and my work. What I have learned through a stack of personal experiences is that those of us who have carved out our own destiny, created something out of nothing, or found a way of living our dreams do three things *very* differently from other people.

The commonality is that we:

- Feel differently
- Think differently
- Act differently

These differences are plentiful, and this short-read catalogs, organizes, and sequences the exact feelings, thoughts, and actions that both I and many of my clients have repeated to achieve our own versions of success. These ingredients make up our contracts with ourselves and, once executed, create the unique and exact formulae to allow the success we have imagined to appear in our real lives.

Exactly Where to Start is your playbook to help you turn a great idea into something great.

1
Getting Started

You picked up this book because you have an idea about something that you have been meaning to start on, have been thinking about working on, and you believe is something that will work well. I expect that this idea has lived in you for some time and for one reason or another you have just failed to get started.

You have also, no doubt, met dozens of people on your journey who "nearly" achieved something, had a "great idea," and failed to bring it to reality for one reason or another. These are the "if only ..." people...

- If only I had started working for myself
- If only I had started earlier
- If only I had listened to the early advice
- If only I were brave enough to try

We have all heard the stories, and perhaps you have told a few of these yourself?

I never planned on writing this book. In fact it was certainly not my *big* idea to make this a reality. It is because of the plethora of requests from people I have met on my journey as an entrepreneur. They have asked me question after question about the precise steps involved in going from an idea to a real-life business. When I shared this fact with my publishers, they quickly responded by suggesting I reply to those questions with this book.

Why me? If you don't know me, my start is from quite humble beginnings. I am the son of a builder, with nothing more than a high school education, and have never once been delivered a handout, secured external financing, or waited for the perfect moment to make something happen. Since starting my first business at the age of 14, I have both successfully and unsuccessfully created and launched hundreds of commercial ventures and ideas and also gone on to help many clients to do the same. In short, I don't ask "Why me?" I ask "Why not me?"

There have been many, many books written about making things happen and getting things done, but none quite like this. You are reading a precise blueprint with the EXACT steps and the EXACT processes required to bring your BIG idea to life. This is exactly the journey used repeatedly throughout my experience to create something out of nothing, turn ideas into reality. And they are the steps I still use today to launch every new product, business initiative, and project.

Regular questions that have been fired in my direction have started to have an air of repetitiveness, and the general direction goes something like this:

- Where can I learn how to do it?
- Why has someone else not done it already?
- What is the right order to do things in?
- When is the right time to do it?
- What happens if it goes wrong?
- Who did it for you?
- How do you fit everything in?

While these are posed as questions, they sound more like excuses or statements of regret. This book is your instruction manual to help you give up on excuses and bypass regret to bring you out on the other side.

There is a good chance that you have already become well practiced at finding reasons not to start. Perhaps you have even worked harder on the excuses than you have on the idea itself. Let's not have it that the catalyst for action that you need is someone else's success with your idea. Let's get started right now.

It is possible that you already have the feeling that I may have some understanding of your situation. You see, the truth is that I have stood in your shoes on many occasions and have a strong belief that I know much of what you are thinking. The reason I know this is that I think it, too. I experience the same feelings of being overwhelmed, the anxieties of uncertainty, and the myriad choices that can very easily leave you paralyzed, unable to take action. These are normal feelings. Not doing something about it is the problem.

I have felt these exact same feelings with every major project, program, or company I have launched; even though many have been successful ideas, there still are these feelings—each and every time. I am unable to make them disappear. They are a simply part of the journey … not a red light. That's why the only way I have managed to facilitate them is to create systems and processes to work around them, overcome the complexities of human emotion, and create non-negotiable checkpoints that have the ability to drag me across the start line and propel me into the game.

Like any BIG idea, writing a book is always a daunting task, this book even more so. This is creating a BIG idea about how to create a BIG idea. The only way to approach this very task was to pull from my years of experience and rely on the exact process that I am writing about to create the book you are currently holding. That took this book writing process from six months down to six weeks!

With my process in place, I half laughed as I looked down at the first blank page to start this book. Because, like you, that first blank page of your next chapter weighs heavy, and stepping into it requires a few moments of courage.

Perhaps what differentiates me from you here is that with years of spectacular successes, ferocious failures, and a lifetime of lessons, you learn to trust the process. Because of this, the process I have used to create this book is the very process the book explains. What you are reading is an example of it, a product of its product, and entrusting this process to complete this piece, ahead of schedule and to a level that I am immensely proud of, is testimony to its application.

If you have read any of my previous work, you will know that my style is very action-focused, with applicable strategies that can be instantly implemented. This read is no different. Accompany your read with the ability to take notes, turn those notes into actions, and you too will know *Exactly Where to Start.*

Here is a quick secret. There is zero need for you to worry about the exact starting point of your BIG idea; you have already started. Even at this point you are already in motion, and your choice is whether to fuel its success or just go about your regular day and forget about it. The start line is already in your rear-view mirror, and some more good news is that there's no finish line either.

Your Action Step
Letter to Self

This is your first commitment to make. If you are moving forward with this idea, then now is your moment to decide to decide. Is this thing happening? Yes or No? Of course, you can decide not to do it; that's an empowering choice, too. It is OK to choose to give up on something or to let it go; it's also essential that if you choose to do something, that you commit to that choice. Nobody learned to swim standing poolside, nobody became a rock star without picking up an instrument, and nobody climbed a mountain without taking a first step.

Action and accountability drive results, and this has led me to understand that people take action in only two areas of their lives:

1. The things they enjoy doing
2. The things they are checked on

Being as this is your idea, my guess is that there are not many people checking in on you. Your task involves you setting a precise deadline today for the date in which your first major checkpoint will be reached. When your deadline is set, take a blank sheet of paper and write yourself a letter by hand. The letter goes like this:

Dear [Insert your name]

Today is [insert date of completion], and I am really proud of you because of all that you have achieved.

I am amazed that you have successfully [insert the successes you plan for].

No doubt you feel [describe the feelings].

You are the inspiration to my life, and without you I would have nothing. Thank you for everything that you do, and I am excited about our future!

Lots of Love,

[Insert your name]

Having completed the letter, place it in a self-addressed envelope and entrust it to a loved one who will mail it back to you on the deadline day you have set.

PHILosophy ────────

"Starting is the hardest task of all. It's not all downhill from here, **but being brave enough to start is all the chance that you need, and once you master the ability to make a start, you have earned the ability to start over as many times as you desire."**

@philmjonesuk

────────

12

2
Stop Waiting for Permission

Back in 2006, I remember a very specific moment when I sat around a dining table with a group of people I was close to at the time. During the conversation, I was sharing some of my visions for the future, plans for growth, and how I saw my future life shaping up. For many, my ambition may have been a little lofty, for the majority it may have seen overly optimistic; but the very specific feedback I received scarred me permanently. And worse still, these words came from the very people that i believed where my supporters, my friends and on my side.

The feedback was the words "My goodness, Phil, you're such a dreamer"—as if it were a bad thing. It was the ripple of giggles that accompanied that really got under my skin. You see, a dream is ambiguous, perhaps even out of control and maybe even something that "just happens"; that was not how I saw my future at all. I was dreaming with my eyes open, making plans, and taking action. I was doing the things I had always done.

I found myself questioning a lot about myself, my thinking, and my life in general. This moment was to become a catalyst for change in my life as I made a giant discovery: I was looking for validation, perhaps even permission from those around me, that I was heading in the right direction. But here's the catch: Most people cannot believe in something that is new, different, or unlike them. That took me a long time to realize.

When stuck at an amber light in our lives it becomes very natural to seek the encouragement, acceptance, and agreement of others toward our goals. This desire for permission can easily create a giant roadblock and add fuel to the negative voice of self-doubt.

Self-doubt can be easily identified if any of these thoughts have occurred to you:

- People will laugh at me.
- It will probably fail anyway.
- I am not ready yet.
- I am too busy to do this now.
- I don't know how to do it.
- It's too expensive.

The trouble with these thoughts is that they move the responsibility for the creation of your desired success out of your hands and toward a fictitious external source. By speaking these types of statements (even if only in your head), you are looking for concrete excuses for why this cannot work and developing limiting self-beliefs toward any impact you personally can have on your outcome.

The mind is a dangerous thing, and it was the great Henry Ford who famously said, "Whether you think you can or you think you can't—you're right." This could not be truer than at this precise moment. Your self-esteem is a powerful asset in your progress, and being kind to it, protecting it, and giving it the fuel it needs, you gain a handsome ally that remains committed to you and your task.

You have the choice to see a roadblock as a dead end or a diversion. Many things in our lives we cannot change, but how we think about those things is always in our complete control. The second you start thinking differently about your obstacles, you empower movement in your actions, and this movement results in opportunities being realized. You can create the catalyst to this movement easily by changing the statements you are making into questions and putting control of the situation back where it belongs—with YOU!

Borrowing some psychology from my earlier book, *Exactly What to Say*, an ideal preface to these questions are the words "What needs to happen to ..." or "What happens if... ?"

When you change the statements above into active questions, you can engage the creative, problem-solving part of your mind. You move from how most people think and toward EXACTLY how you should think:

- What happens if people laugh at me?
- What happens if it fails?
- What needs to happen for me to feel ready?
- What needs to happen for me to prioritize this?
- What needs to happen for me to learn the missing skills?
- What needs to happen for me to raise the funds to start?

Taking the positive step of turning your problems into challenges and your limiting beliefs into puzzles, you very quickly create a natural road map of progressive steps. These allow you to take complete control of your own circumstances.

Steve Jobs once said, "It is not our customers' responsibility to know what they want." That exact thinking gave birth to the iPad. If you have a BIG idea, then it is your responsibility to move forward with it. Nobody else has to do the work, nobody else needs to believe in you, and nobody else will be the benefactor of your success more than you will be.

Your Action Step
Done-It List

Regardless of how you feel, the truth is that you are already a proven success story. Since an early age, you have been achieving things while many of those successes are buried in your memory. It is therefore easy to feel displaced by the overwhelming tasks you need to conquer. As you track back over your life, consider the multitude of achievements and accolades you have collected. If you review the history of sports, you will find many stories showing that to be a winner you have to feel like a winner—and that success breeds success. Your task right now is to tap into some of your historic successes. Regardless of how far you need to go back, invest some time in building yourself up and reliving some of the proud moments from your history.

There was once a time in your life where tasks like walking, tying your shoelaces, and cursive writing all seemed impossible. Since that time, your own successes have been plentiful and week in, week out, you have been cataloging victories—often forgetting to even notice what you succeed at.

Before crafting this book, I drafted a physical list of more than 200 specific business initiatives or BIG ideas I have recorded success in, and when I finished my confidence of my ability to write this book had moved significantly upward.

Some of the successes were as far back as high school and others were as recent as last week. I didn't rank them, place them in date order, or sequence in any way. I just took an hour or so and had fun listing all the historic successes I had experienced making something happen in my life. On reflection, some seemed really trivial (I listed the fact that I designed and built a piece of furniture in my woodworking class) and others were more profound (the runaway success of my first Audible release). The size of the success was irrelevant, as the purpose of the exercise was to prove that success is something that I had a proven track record in.

Craft your list, document your successes, and be kind to yourself in the process. The moment you document just how many challenges you have overcome in the past, you will realize that you have a rich history of overcoming adversity and the task at hand starts to feel a lot more doable.

PHILosophy _____

"In the moments when you question your abilities and ask yourself whether you can really do it.... **Please remind yourself all of the impossible feats you have already conquered.**

If you spent as much effort building on your successes as you did fueling your failures, imagine the difference it would make."

@philmjonesuk

3
Stare Down the Monster

As people, a natural reaction for many is to see things as either far worse or far better than reality. This overexertion or dramatization of a situation is often just an internal defense mechanism to deliver weight to the argument.

In my history, I have witnessed examples of complete ignorance that have resulted in a BIG idea having zero chance of success because of dramatically unrealistic expectations, as well as even more examples of individuals potentially seeing outcomes far worse than reality and obsessing about problems that don't really exist.

Assuming you are not one of the many who fail to start, when approaching a new venture there are just two common approaches that can have calamitous consequences.

First: Blind Optimism

Trying to succeed at a long-term plan without care or consequence and the assumption that everything will work out just fine may have been the success formulae for a handful of ventures, but it's laced with giant risk and unnecessarily irresponsible. This approach of hopeful naivety leaves you perfectly positioned for a giant dose of crippling disappointment. By seeing nothing but the best for the success of the venture, you can easily underestimate the task and rely on a single strategy (getting lucky) that the casino industry has proved will fail for the player far more often than it will succeed.

Second: Paralyzing Fear

Change is scary, and the unknown can be a frightening place. What happens though is that, as you fuel the fear, you start to fertilize the hurdles ahead of you and dramatize every single thing that could go wrong. Mole hills become mountains and you rapidly become overwhelmed by the task ahead, resulting in an inability to progress. I am sure that there are millions of BIG ideas that failed to make progress because of this destructive belief.

The Alternative: Useful Truth

Taking the time to plan, organize, and gain clarity over the size of the challenge sets you up differently. Seeing things exactly as they are is a solid and powerful position to begin from. It's level-headed and grounded, often anchored in experience, although this experience is often borrowed from others, modeled from similar BIG ideas, and laced in realism. Understanding the consequences of failure, the potential of success, and what it might take is a solid position from which to leap forward into creating a new reality.

What we are talking about is calculating the risk and reward before diving in. It's easy to get excited about the upward potential, but the realization of the potential downsides becomes even more empowering.

At this time, it is your responsibility to explore the risks and discover the truth of what really could go wrong. Obviously, there is a giant difference between a BIG idea that requires you to quit your job, refinance your house, and invest your life savings and a desire to turn a passion into profit by starting a home-based business.

Getting to this position of "useful truth" is both harder than it sounds and easier than it looks. My process is always to push the BIG idea through the funnel of six powerful questions.

Question 1. Is It Possible?

Spending too long on this question can easily lead to analysis paralysis. All I am looking for is a simple yes or no to the potential viability of the idea. It can sometimes be easiest to answer this by finding an example of something similar that has been realized. Seeing evidence of others succeeding before you is proof that a market exists and not necessarily that a market is saturated. Your opportunity lies in bringing your difference to that existing market.

A friend of mine wanted to quit her job and start a home-based beauty business. Within a few minutes of searching, it was obvious that the possibility of this becoming real was positive, with dozens of examples of others who had achieved similar dreams.

Question 2. How Can I Prove Concept?

Before something can be a long-term success, it needs to be a one-time success. What needs to happen for you to create a genuine trial of your idea and gain the confidence that it can really go the distance? Don't over-think the answer—there are plenty of correct options—pick one that feels good to you.

EXAMPLE

A client wanted to launch an online training program to serve young people who felt stuck in the wrong careers. The goal was for it to be an automated course delivered through video tutorials that students could access in their own time. Before going to the expense of designing, building, and marketing the online program, I advised my client first to test the content with a small group of paying clients by delivering the training personally over a video conference platform and measure the results, gather feedback, and test the program. The result was that the concept was tested, resulting in testimonials and increased confidence in there being a solid market for the content. What's more, the content and product evolved a little from the experience of a user group trial.

Question 3. What Is the Worst That Could Happen?

Possibly the most important and most liberating question of all is this one. The ability truly and honestly to look at the potential risk of attempting to bring a BIG idea to life often gives you the confidence and freedom to work harder for its success.

Look at what could go wrong and accept and understand those consequences. Your fears of the risks could be the biggest barrier to you starting. Taking a very honest look at the specific risks associated with the BIG idea can help you realize that you are more in control than you thought you were.

EXAMPLE

A common example I experience is people who want to quit their jobs to chase their BIG ideas and who are fearful of being without an income and of losing everything. With one particular client who dreamed of becoming a full-time business consultant but needed to leave his well-paid job to do so, I advised him to secure a single, retainer-based client who covered his household expenses and still allowed him time to find more clients. This gave him the confidence and freedom to take the risk. Then, looking at his worst case scenario, we considered whether he needed re-employment if his venture failed, and he felt confident he could be re-employed in no longer than six months. With more than six months of overhead in personal savings and one client secured, he leaped forward into his new career with added confidence.

Question 4. How Will I Feel Upon Achieving Success?

Emotions trigger more decisions than logic ever will. Something must always "feel right" before it will ever "make sense," and this is as true in the conversations we have with ourselves as it is with those we have with others. Familiar positive feelings become addictive and have the ability to make us desire more of them in our lives. By considering the way you will feel upon achieving success with your BIG idea, you create something real in your emotional memory that, once felt, you feel the need to chase after. For something to exist in your future, without accident and by design, you must first imagine that scenario and enjoy the fruits of your labor, even if only hypo- thetically and just for a moment.

EXAMPLE

I met a young student at a seminar once who had a dream of opening his own hearing care practice in Nashville, Tennessee, following graduation. I spent some time with him and had him talk me through his vision of serving only musicians, increasing awareness locally of the risks of excessive noise for musicians, and providing education to prevent future hearing issues. He described the look of his office, right down to the memorabilia hanging on the wall. I asked him to imagine himself opening that office in a few years and having a thriving local business, and then asked him how he would feel if that were all true. In the answers to such questions lies the magic. I am 100 percent certain that he is now more likely to realize his BIG idea, having taken the time to imagine how it felt first.

Question 5. Can I Make a Game of It?

There is a very high probability that achieving your BIG idea requires more than a little hard work. At times, it may feel overwhelming and perhaps even too hard. Enjoyment fuels productivity and, given that, people only do two things in life:

- What they enjoy doing
- What they get checked on

Given this, anything we can do to make the task more fun is bound to help. Now I have no idea what makes something fun to you, but when I was at school I renamed my exams and tests as puzzles and quizzes. This is your moment to play, add some entertainment to the process, and plan in things that make you smile or gamify your journey. On occasion, this may be harder than you think; don't give up on this question, you will need the answers to help you go the distance.

EXAMPLE

The book-writing process can be mind-numbing and challenging. Organizing thoughts, ideas, stories, and examples into a seamless arc and then packaging it neatly together with a continuous, reassuring, and confident tone has its challenges. Having helped dozens of people to become published, I have found a tiny tip that has added a little bonus fun to the process—the tracking process. On many occasions, I have created walls of colored Post-its with different colors representing different components of the work. These notes can then be moved around a whiteboard of chapter headings to create a perfect flow for the manuscript. The color pattern and mix helps me visualize the blend of content, the sequencing gives me the order, and the best thing, as each part is written the wall of Post-its gets smaller and I can physically see my progress.

———————

Question 6. What's the First Step?

It is hard to know the first thing to do, and there are many possible answers here. My advice is to gain clarity by answering two powerful questions:

- Who are the people you want to serve?
- What are the challenges you plan to help them overcome?

In the answers to these questions you will find your focus and learn what direction to go. Too many people spend all their energy working toward what they would "like to do," when the real question should be "Who do you want to help?" Laser-focused vision on what you truly want to achieve is essential to prevent future distractions and confirm viability of the idea.

EXAMPLE

A request I often receive is how to start in the business of becoming a professional or motivational speaker. It can be seen as a glamorous profession and can seem very attractive from the outside world. The ability to speak on stage is only part of the job; the bigger part is having an audience to serve. Without an audience, your stagecraft remains useless. An aspiring speaker had this same challenge and came to me looking for guidance. In one short conversation, he moved from being a "marketing speaker" to a speaker who helps busy accountants find more clients with social media.

One other big truth for you realize is that your energy spent on your BIG idea will have negative consequences elsewhere. There is no doubt that as your attention is focused in this area it is removed from somewhere else and could potentially leave you conflicted. Be aware that you are 100 percent capable of achieving many different things; it is, however, impossible for you to achieve *every* given thing, so choose wisely.

Your Action Step

Discover the Answers to Six Powerful Questions

Entering into this venture with your eyes open and your senses clear gives you a productive starting place. Your focus is on "getting started" and not "being finished," so please take enough time to understand the difference between perceived risk and true constraints.

Grab your notebook and set to work on documenting your answers to the six powerful questions, providing enough evidence for each answer to make you feel stronger about getting started.

1. Is it possible?
2. How can I prove concept?
3. What is the worst that could happen?
4. How will I feel upon achieving success?
5. Can I make a game of it?
6. What's the first step?

Working through these questions with a trusted associate may add an improved dynamic to the process and a little extra accountability. Be sure to choose a person looking for his or her support and not negativity. Remember the "dreamer" story from Chapter 2?

_____

PHILosophy ———

"To reach the top then start by raising the bottom. **It gives you something to stand on!"**
@philmjonesuk

———

4

Make It Work on Paper

The possibilities for your ideas to become real are somewhere near endless. Having a "yes or no" answer to the possibility of success empowers progress, but does not really start you moving. For example, Knowing that traveling around the Amalfi Coast is possible allows you to imagine the experience, yet without added details, potential is the only progress that you make. The idea remains nothing more real than the hypothetical truth and your knowledge in its potential is humbling for a moment yet paralyzing over time.

I believe that this is a mistake that many make when deciding to move forward with their BIG ideas. They accept the possibility, yet fail to consider the precise steps or checkpoints to make realistic progress.

My reason for mentioning the Amalfi Coast trip is because it is the exact trip a friend of mine named Brandy is longing to take. Listening to her talk about it is always a joy as she shares the dozens of activities planned to fit into a magical four-day trip. As I was listening to her I found myself doing the mathematics on the proposed adventure. It was very clear to me when adding up the time required to make the dream a reality that the proposed adventure was either completely impossible to deliver or required light speed transportation and zero time at each activity.

I ask here for you to become beautifully realistic with your ambitious plans and ensure that the goal you are looking to achieve actually is possible. For a business idea to be viable, it typically needs to be successful in the following areas:

- Startup-able: Enough money to build it
- Sustainable: Makes enough to go the distance
- Profitable: Makes more than is spends
- Exitable: Can be stopped or passed on to others

Start with an end in mind and identify exactly what you want to achieve. It is not enough to simply label what you want to achieve; join the dots and color the gaps with the details of the economic successes you are planning to achieve.

The goal of this step is to be able to progress significantly along the path of making your idea a reality. Plan it in a way that everything adds up and is worth doing. It's highly unlikely that you would consider making a new dish without a recipe and ingredients list to follow, take a long journey without planning a route, or start building a house without a solid set of realistic plans. The same is true with launching your BIG idea.

Let's work with an example for someone who wants to open a coffee shop.

Change your internal and external conversation from … "I plan to open a coffee shop in the local town" and evolve this statement into a considered set of thoughts like …

I am planning to open a small coffee shop on Main Street next January. It will provide high-quality artisan hot drinks to commuters and tourists, and I expect to sell around 3,500 cups a week at an average $3 a cup. This means that the revenue from coffee alone will be $10,500 a week, or around $546,000 a year. Each cup of coffee will cost me around 50 cents, so my cost of goods is expected to be approximately $90,000 annually, which reduces my gross profit to somewhere near $450,000 for the year. I have looked at rents and rates. My expenses would be around $10,000 a month and additional help and staff will be around the same. These expenses reduce profit to around $260,000, and then there are a number of incidentals that I am sure could run to another $60,000 or so a year. My current salary in my job is $80,000 a year, so it seems that if I can make this work then I will be making more money and having much more fun. I am currently working on raising the $70,000 it will cost me to get started.

What you should notice from this example is that there are lots of approximations, guesses, and hypotheses—all considered with some reasonable research.

Before analysis paralysis sets in, it's important to have an elevated view of what success might look like. Almost every successful entrepreneur I have met can simply and easily articulate the basic financial model for his or her success and communicate it in ways that others can understand.

Working toward a clear model is an essential step that, if you fail to give attention to it, could have you starting a venture that is destined to fail before you even start.

In my mind, every commercial venture should start with at least working knowledge of the answers to the following questions:

- How many customers?
- Paying how much money?
- How often will they visit?
- At what expense?
- What are your ongoing liabilities?
- How much will it cost to get started?

Once you have answers to these questions documented, then be brave enough to check your assumptions. The coffee shop example makes some bold assumptions, the largest probably the 3,500 cups of coffee per week. I created this number by spending time in a local coffee shop, both off peak and at a peak time and physically counted the numbers of cups produced.

In a busy hour, they produced around 150 cups and in a slow hour more like 30. I decided to pick a median of around 50 cups an hour for ten hours a day across a seven-day week, which gave me the 3,500 number to work with. It is unlikely that this type of estimate will ever be perfect. The goal at this stage is to build your model using the power of the "educated guess."

Experience has given me three main strategies to make educated guesses with increased levels of accuracy:

- **Observe.** Where can you visit to watch someone else doing what you want to do?
- **Ask.** Find others who have already achieved similar objectives to what you are hoping to achieve and ask them your questions.
- **Investigate.** Research in books, online articles, and supplier catalogs to find the information you require. With so much information just a click away, there are few excuses for unanswered questions.

Doing your research requires work. Many avoid the work, and it could be your biggest barrier to achieving your goal. As you gather the information you need, more questions will come up, and as you uncover more and more answers you will start to gain the clarity necessary to make real choices. It is not uncommon for people to decide to give up at this stage as they find the truth and the reality crushes the dream. My perception on this is that it is better to choose consciously to *not* do something based on some research before you get too far into it than to naively start and find out too late that it won't work out.

It's also highly probable that as you begin to make your idea work on paper your ambition will be fueled and the possibilities will become more plentiful. In this case, overcoming obstacles seems more achievable and your vision sharpens to a point of heightened belief in your idea becoming reality.

When I invited Brandy to make her Amalfi Coast trip "work on paper," she discovered the best time of year to visit, choose three specific places to stay, shortlisted the exact excursions she wanted to take, and brought the whole thing in on budget. The result is that the trip is now scheduled and booked.

Your Action Step

Document Your Plan

Now it's your turn to have your plan written down with dates, constraints, forecasts, and assumptions clearly documented and considered. Bring your BIG idea to life and create a working model of its existence. Observe others who have achieved something similar, ask questions of those who can give you answers, and investigate to ensure that you have complete clarity about what you are doing. Be ready, ready, ready to answer the questions below with confidence, posture, and accuracy.

What do you want to achieve?

Can you bring it to life with color, adjectives, passion, and enthusiasm so that others can clearly see what you can see?

By when will you have achieved it?

Do you have a definite deadline or checkpoint that you are working toward?

How is it going to work?

Can you articulate a basic financial model that proves you understand what it will take to get started, what it will cost to achieve it, and what its success can deliver?

You have my permission to document this however you choose, as long as you physically lift the vision from your mind and re-create it in a document, presentation, picture, or report that makes sense to others. Only after you have the clarity that allows your idea to be shared with others will you have sufficient clarity to make it into reality.

PHILosophy ——————

"If it doesn't work on paper, then it has zero chance in reality. It's easier to tear up a piece of paper than it is to rebuild a life."

@philmjonesuk

——————

5

Give Yourself a Fine Reputation to Live Up To

Early in my career I was fortunate enough to have studied the work of the great Dale Carnegie. One very specific lesson, when shared, hit me so hard that it stopped me in my tracks and etched itself onto me for every day that has followed. It was a management lesson about getting more from others, the point being "to give others a fine reputation to live up to." In its original form this lesson made perfect sense, and its application was bountiful, as it encourages me to see more for others than sometimes they see for themselves—and to show that I expect more from people by the language I share about them.

Simply put, if I would state in public that Sarah has made great progress in her sales numbers, then the likelihood would be that Sarah would continue to make great progress in her sales numbers. If I stated that Alan has always been a great resource for others who have found the internal computer system difficult to work with, then the likelihood would be that Alan would continue in that capacity, or perhaps even more so, make himself available.

My real learning was, though, the ability to apply this piece of advice to myself. Seeing how well it worked to manage and lead others, I figured that it might have the exact same power if applied to me. From that moment, I have started to take the responsibility and create the liability of giving myself a fine reputation to live up to.

Through the years, humans have repeatedly provided us with examples of rising to the occasion when the occasion is presented to us. My thoughts have always been on how I can create an occasion worth rising for.

A clear example of this was the creation of my first book, *Toolbox*. I knew that I wanted to write a book. I felt confident I had enough to say, and I also had the belief that I could easily put this task off month after month and never fulfill its possibility.

Taking this knowledge, fueled by the reframed lesson from Carnegie, I set out with a number of steps that turned a "good idea" into a "nonnegotiable reality."

Step 1. Ask for Help

With any BIG idea, you will find that there are a large number of people who will support you on your quest. The second you decide you are doing something, then start to communicate your need for input from others. There is one thing that everyone loves to give—an opinion. Before the launch of my first book, in the early stages, I asked groups of people for input and suggestions on titles, subtitles, the content, cover designs, and more. Involving others not only provides you with valuable insight and support, but also flips a switch in your own mind that this is now happening.

Step 2. Social Accountability

It's time to announce your plans to the world ahead of time and share what is happening and when it will be complete. The responsibility attached to making something public provides you the motivation to not let your reputation down. You know that those you share the news with may ask questions on your progress and check in on your timeline. Not having good answers to their inquiries could prove to be a little embarrassing. You may feel nervous or anxious at this stage. Be brave and share with your world that your BIG idea is about to become very real. For me this was sharing the confirmed book cover across all social platforms with a release date for the book, all before I had even written a complete chapter!!!

Step 3. Sell It First

There is nothing more powerful to drive production than the added accountability of paying customers. Following the introduction of the cover design, my next move was to advertise its release and look for pre-orders for the book. Having a few hundred people who had already committed their hard-earned money for the book created a few very important emotions. Of course, the thought of needing to refund these people's money was more painful than the work required to complete the book. Bigger than that was the confidence that at least a few people where interested in actually reading my ramblings. This added confidence of knowing with certainty that there is a genuine market for what you are doing is the perfect confidence-boosting motivator to help you get to work.

Step 4. Levels of Success

Success in anything should never be considered to be a specific or definitive place. At this point, I would take what I am working on and create three very vivid checkpoints for success that mitigate my possibility of failure. Defining success at specific levels keeps you in control, protects your emotions, and also encourages optimism.

First level: Worst case scenario
Second level: My realistic goal
Third level: Utopia

For the first book, level one was me producing a finished book that I could hold in my hand, give to my Mum (yes, that is how we spell Mom in the UK), and feel proud of being a published author. The second level was that I would share it through my events, and people would actually purchase the book to a point of me making a profit and gain at least 10 positive reviews from readers. The third level was that I would wake up one morning and the book had been a viral sensation, selling thousands of copies overnight and becoming an international bestseller.

Having this realigned set of expectations provides you with certainty the venture will be successful, clarity over your objectives, and a ridiculous goal to chase and keep the dream alive.

Giving yourself a fine reputation to live up to changes the probability of your ability to complete your goal from very possible to highly probable, and without this thought process I am certain that dozens of my ideas would never have made their way to reality.

Your Action Step
Make a Press Release

At this exact moment, while you are feeling inspired to do so, your job is to make a very public announcement of your plans and by when they will be achieved. If you choose to make this announcement via social media, then feel free to use the #exactlywheretostart or tag me personally and I may even have some words of advice or encouragement to help you on your way.

PHILosophy ———

"Nothing happens unless YOU make it happen. **Give YOURSELF a fine reputation to live up to.**"

@philmjonesuk

———

6
Build Your Squad

In the second chapter of this book I shared with you the "dreamer" story and the impact that moment had on my life. Since that point I have consciously been involved in conversations with many people and realized that the very conversation was becoming destructive to my own personal vision and confidence to achieve it.

One particular repetitive conversation was one I had with some family members as I was building the very life business that I have today. The early days of me building a business came at a time when the economy was in a state of disrepair, my personal life was in tatters, and every day we would read press headlines of another failed business. Things got very tight for me, and many of life's luxuries that were once the norm for me now seemed huge extravagances and on many occasions where completely out of reach. At one point, I remember things being so tight that I would fill my car with fuel certain that all my cards would be declined, and I had no other means to pay.

Even worse at this point in my life was that my business was actually doing great; I was just suffering from the economic challenges of bad decisions and the growing pains of challenging cash flow.

During this time period whenever I spoke with family members, their love poured out with unqualified wisdom, advising me to get a job, and on some occasions even sharing specific vacancies they had sourced on my behalf.

Internally, their expressions of care, concern, and worry was received as though even my family did not believe in me. This weighed really heavily on me, and for periods made me question everything.

The realization that opened the floodgates for some of the biggest growth in my life and my business was that I was using the right people for the wrong things in my life, and I had a huge number of vacancies. I was asking my mother to be my career advisor, my sister to be my business coach, and one of my employees to be my best friend. I had good people in completely wrong roles in my life. There was no way that my mother could offer me valuable advice to shape my financial future; she has been a brilliant mother since I have known her and a valuable employee at the garden center where she works, but never had she had to navigate the challenges I was being faced with at that time, nor was it fair that I expected her to do so.

This was a revelation to me. I needed to change the roles I had for some of the key people in my life and then build the squad I needed to support my next steps. Conversations with my family soon became contained to fun and light-hearted engagements that delivered me valuable respite from my work life and, one by one, I made life-altering decisions from adding and subtracting people from my life.

Cheerleaders.– Encouragement, recognition, and celebration partners are required to feed our need for significance. Being surrounded by people who want to see you win can make all the difference in helping you to succeed. Work hard to collect people in this role and grab every opportunity you can to fill this role for others.

Role Models. Success certainly leaves clues, and finding specific people who are ahead of you in your journey with a proven track record of achieving something like what you are shooting for gives you a journey to study, follow, and learn from. Even from a distance you can learn so much if you are prepared to find the truth in their stories and not just admire them from afar.

Mentors. A mentor can give even more than a role model, as a mentor is likely to share his or her own experience with you to help you make better decisions. It is your responsibility to choose a mentor and not his or hers to choose you. Find people you can access who have experience you would like to borrow, and work to learn from them.

Coaches. Unlike a mentor, a great coach is less about guiding you with advice and experience and more about asking you the questions you have not yet asked yourself. Coaches can change the way you think, ensure you do the things you say you are going to do, and also pick you up when you fall down.

Trainers. There is no way that you currently know all you need to know to succeed with your BIG idea. If there are skills you are missing, then identify the trainers who can teach you what you need to know.

Resources. No squad is complete without a number of people working behind the scenes and completing tasks that are not in your skillset and still need to be done. For me these are web development, graphic design, printing, travel planning, and much, much more. Allocating other trusted people allows you to spend your time doing what you are good at and keeps the momentum going.

Advisors. There is no way that you are expected to know all that you need to know as you progress with your BIG idea. Collect trusted advisors who can respond to questions, talk over situations, and mitigate risk. I have dozens in this role and could not succeed without them.

Aspirational Peers. Possibly the most important group are those who are on a similar journey to yours and who inspire you. These people can typically play many of the roles listed above and, in my opinion, are the most important to surround yourself with.

All of these people will start to make themselves available to you when you invest the time to look for them. The best place to start is by finding groups of your aspirational peers. These groups exist in abundance in the form of networking groups, online communities, training courses, conferences, and exhibitions. Your goal is to find your people and have those people come into your life in ways that inspire, encourage, educate, empower, and enable you to achieve.

Doing something for yourself does not mean that you should do it by yourself. We all need a team of cheerleaders, role models, mentors, coaches, and advisors.

A word of warning. As you let more people into your life, please understand the profound difference between advice and opinion. It can be very easy to confuse the two, and often opinion is disguised as advice. Both are valuable, yet confusing one for the other can have disastrous consequences. The key to understanding the difference is to question the specific experience of the person whose thoughts are being shared with you. If based on precise, first-hand experience, I will typically receive the information as advice. If the thoughts shared with me are based on a person's hypothetical knowledge of the scenario, then I will treat it as an opinion.

Your Action Step

Complete a Life Laundry

This may sound crude, and as you work through this step you may have some very difficult decisions to make.

I am asking you to work through three exact steps.

Step 1. Human Audit

Clearly define the roles of the key people in your
life and ensure those roles are constructive for
your future success plans. After defined their
roles, communicate clearly with those people
how best they can support you in your success
plans. If you have people in your life who have
a destructive effect on your life, then take
steps to remove or reduce the impact they
have on your life.

Step 2. Identify Your Missing People

Review the people categories mentioned above and gain clarity on the exact roles that need to be filled. You may also list potential candidates from your extended network whom you would like to have in those roles.

Step 3. Actively Fill the Vacancies

Attend events, join groups, and reach out to individuals who can help you build the network you want to be surrounded by. This may require further investment of time and money, and it's a relentless and lifelong task if you continue to set new goals. Keep building your squad.

PHILosophy ————

"If someone else can do it,
then can someone else
be me?"

@philmjonesuk

————

7 Progress Beats Perfection

Almost every successful business, project, product, or service is still a very long way from being its perfect self, but still it is easy to sit back and marvel at their awesomeness. Think about the businesses you admire and give thought to exactly how they started.

Every Michelin-starred chef had to first learn how to cook an egg, every talented guitarist learned the basic notes, and every global traveler at some point was waiting for a bus. I would go as far to say that every individual or company that you admire is not only far from perfect, but also started out from some very humble beginnings. Do your homework on every one of your role models, and more often or not, you will find that they started as a boy or a girl with the ambition to start and move slightly quicker than the rest of the herd, reach a little higher than the others, and stretch themselves to keep growing with a sprinkling more tenacity.

A piece of advice I was fortunate enough to collect was that "good is often good enough." Before something can be described as brilliant, it first needs to exist, and once it exists it can then be improved.

I am almost certain that everything you plan will turn out different from the way you expect it to. It is an almost certainty that things will go wrong and failures will appear in immeasurable quantities as you progress. Failing is something that many people live in fear of, yet the relentless failings of others have created almost every major accomplishment the world has ever seen.

To help you wrap your head around this, first understand the difference between a failure and a mistake:

- A *mistake* is incorrectly doing something that you knew specifically how you were supposed to do.
- A *failure* is trying something you have not tried before and it working out differently than you hoped for.

Seeing these differences instantly empowers a difference in your acceptance between the two and possibly helps you become more excited about your future failures.

Your responsibility at this point of your journey is to fail fast, fail often, and where possible, fail forward. Once failure becomes something you embrace and don't allow to entangle you, then your progress starts to speed up. The failures create knowledge, the knowledge empowers decisions, the decisions create actions, and the actions create progress.

It would be a huge disappointment to your future self if your BIG idea remained just that. The action steps required to get from where you are now to accomplishing what you want can certainly feel overwhelming, and a trusted way to reduce your anxiety is to stop running a giant "to-do" list and replace your plan with some clearly marked checkpoints.

When you focus on what you need to do, you create dozens of tasks that have right and wrong ways of doing each of them, and "perfection paralysis" can sabotage your success.

The alternative means that you take control of what you need to have done and by when. These nonnegotiable checkpoints create the freedom for failure to thrive and progress to prosper. It becomes less about "how" you do something and shifts the emphasis to the desired outcome. Think for a second about the abundance of outcomes that you rely on and for which you have zero knowledge or interest about how those outcomes are achieved.

Examples for me include:

- I need to arrive in Atlanta safely before 10 a.m. tomorrow.

- We have 60 people in a workshop on Friday, and they all will need lunch.

- This book manuscript needs to be submitted by the end of the month.

The options around achieving success in these nonnegotiable outcomes are plentiful. The outcomes themselves are absolute.

Achieving success in your BIG idea is unlikely to be a straight line from where you are now to where you would like to be. There is also no one right way to get there. There are just actions you can take that get you closer and other actions that will take you further away.

When you have the individual checkpoints highlighted, all your activity can drive toward those checkpoints, and achieving your BIG idea can become as progressive as building a piece of flat-packed furniture. The BIG similarity between the progress of your BIG idea and constructing a piece of flat-packed furniture is that to achieve the end result you are looking for it makes sense to go no faster than one step at a time.

Your determined focus should now shift toward nothing other than the next BIG step. At every level, the "next step" is the key to your progress, and the second you focus your efforts on nothing more than achieving your next step, your progress curve quickly escalates.

Let me explain what I mean with some examples of real people I have worked with.

EXAMPLE
The Talented Musician

A young man had been relentless working on his art for years and had the experience of being in the background of a number of local bands. He had been developing his own unique music for months in the safety of his bedroom. The goal was to successfully release his own music and take his act on the road with him becoming a successful front man.

My advice was that before you can successfully deliver hundreds of shows and build an army of raving fans, you must first deliver one show, and learn from that experience. Instead of trying to answer the "How do I become a rock star?" question, the question became how to deliver one show and test the material and the experience.

This change of thought process created sufficient boundaries to find a local venue, confirm a date, collaborate with a couple of artists, and deliver a show to a paying audience. The result was that he then became a successful rock star, with fans enjoying his music—even if just for one night.

The physical experience of this bold step and the collected video and photo evidence have resulted in the band being able to secure more live events, collect more fans, and grow closer to the BIG goal. It started by planning one single event.

———

EXAMPLE
The Cake Maker

A lady approached me who had the passion of baking and wanted to find a way of starting a cake-making business and quit her full-time job. Although she had a lot of experience in making cakes for all occasions, she had zero experience of running a business.

Instead of focusing on building a complete business, we discussed a bold next step, creating three-tiered packaged prices for celebration cakes that allowed her to answer the "Will you make me a cake?" question with an answer that included a price point. She soon had a network utilizing her skills on a regular basis and was being paid for her talents.

By creating a price list for three levels of service, she made it easier for her customers to decide what they wanted and the result was that in the first week she went from having a hobby to having a home-based business. Ten months later, her little part-time thing became so busy that she had the choice to leave her full-time job and build her business full time.

She now runs a very successful business making cakes for a whole host of celebrations, with a shop front, a team of staff, and regular training classes to help others to become better home bakers. It started by creating a price list to allow her to be paid for her passion alongside her existing commitments.

The Unemployed Videographer

I was approached by a friend of a friend of a friend who had recently been made redundant from one of the largest television networks in the UK and was looking to start a business using his skills as a camera man. His skills were broad, and there where dozens of options; the biggest challenge was that he needed to be earning again quickly and make provisions for his loss of income.

I helped him to find clarity over creating a single packaged service for a specific niche of people who had a problem that needed to be solved and who could make a decision quickly. We packaged a service for experts who needed videos for their websites to share what made them different and offer advice to customers and potential customers.

Starting with a single product allowed him to find groups of potential customers more easily and gain their commitment quickly, and within a matter of weeks he was in business.

EXAMPLE
The Undercover Author

A client in a coaching group wanted to publish a book, was overwhelmed by the entire process, and had so much experience she wanted to share that she had no idea where to start.

I helped her realize that her goal might not be limited to publishing a book and could be expanded to the fact that she wanted to publish her experience and expertise in the written word. By helping her realize that she could, in fact, write multiple books, reports, articles, and more, I freed her creativity to start and removed the pressure of one singular piece of brilliance. I advised her to start by writing six short articles that she could publish on her own social media.

Just weeks later she had published the articles, enjoyed the process, and gained feedback from readers. After starting with six articles, she has now found the confidence to work on her first book and is at the point of a completed first draft as I write this sentence.

———

EXAMPLE
The Passionate Parent

When I met this lady, I was blown away by her dedication, enthusiasm, and commitment to supporting and raising awareness of a rare condition that affects a number of children and their ability to learn. She had so much experience to share and had the desire to follow her passion and make a career out of educating others on both the effect of this condition and the impact it can have on the behaviors of people who come into contact with it.

Unsure where to start, we decided that she first required a platform that helped provide trusted, unbiased advice and a professional image through which to approach schools. The first objective was to create a website and a movement that was bigger than one individual and that provided a launch pad for all future actions.

We decided upon to use a crowdsourcing platform to raise the funds to build the website and start the movement. Four weeks after the fund-raising page launched, she had collected enough donations to build the website, create the brand, and do so much more. Better still, she had dozens of supporters who wanted to be kept up-to-date on progress and would become ambassadors for her mission.

Today she has an established nonprofit organization that is making huge progress on the initial goal. It started with being brave enough to launch a fundraising page and ask for help from others.

These real-life scenarios all demonstrate how to start something from nothing, and all indicate the importance of a bold and controlled first step to start the journey. The exact same thought process is used in more established ventures when change or growth is desired.

When the owners of a local fitness studio wanted to franchise the brand and open more locations, the first step I suggested was to develop their existing location with people and systems so that it could run without the owners having any day-to-day responsibility.

When an independent hearing care business wanted to expand and employ more staff, they were fearful of the risk, the expense, and all the "What if's." Instead of worrying about that, I gave them the first step to write job descriptions for themselves and the vacancies and start advertising.

When a large company was planning to launch a new product and was becoming overwhelmed by the workload and fearful of its impact on their market, the first step I gave them was to test the product on their existing customers and see whether those people experienced the proposed improvements.

The goal of a bold next step is the real-world equivalent of testing the temperature of the water before diving in head first. It is more than dipping your toe in; instead it is getting up to your knees in the water, and the benefits of doing so become very clear, very quickly.

As I see it, there are three giant benefits from this approach.

1. **Experience.** By doing something that is concrete and purposeful, you learn very quickly by living the outcomes of your actions.

2. **Confidence.** The experience helps you realize your abilities, and with the feedback of other stakeholders your likelihood for future success grows, even if the experience was not positive.

3. **Accountability.** The step you take makes your idea real and, having started, going back can be a harder choice than moving forward.

There is time for perfection; it's just that time is not now. Drive toward your next big little step and gain the experience, confidence, and accountability to help you go the distance.

Your Action Step

Define and Realize Your First Checkpoint

Now it is your turn to define the exact thing that you need to do to moves you from procrastination into progress. Get specific and create a nonnegotiable next step that you are in control of that moves you a big step closer to your BIG idea becoming a reality. This is not a checkpoint that happens behind the scenes and it has nothing to do with "getting ready" and everything to do with "getting started." Be brave, be bold, and use everything you have learned in this book so far to define a specific, time-bound event that launches you in the right direction. To ensure that your checkpoint meets the success criteria, test it against these three questions:

1. Do you gain real-world experience that grows your knowledge base on your BIG idea?

2. Will the experience result in you having improved confidence in future activities and discussions about your BIG idea?

3. Are other people in your network exposed to your actions, and can they provide accountability and feedback following the activity?

If you can answer "Yes" to these three questions, you have a checkpoint worth driving toward and should probably be making progress on making it real before reading another word!

PHIL**osophy** _____

"To progress you need to know where you are heading and what the next step is—everything else is just a distraction."

@philmjonesuk

_____

8
Indecision Is the Enemy

The power of a river is amplified by the fact that it never rests and never stops moving. A river lacks the ability to procrastinate or ponder, makes bold choices, and does everything in its power to make it to the coast. At each twist and turn in your progress, your success is dependent on your ability to compound the important moments and keep moving forward. With almost every BIG idea that has reached sustainability, you can track back in its history and see that at some point it had the benefit of momentum to drive it. Momentum is your fuel and something you have the ability to influence.

Your success is dependent on your ability to make continued progress at point after point. Consider the simplicity of running on a treadmill. If the goal is to complete the distance of 26.2 miles and run an entire marathon, that goal becomes easier to realize having already run three miles, reached 10 miles, or even when resorting to reducing your run to a jog or a walk. All the time you are moving, your progress is real. The second you stop, the counter starts back from the beginning.

I run on treadmills regularly with the goal of keeping fit while traveling, and a typical dilemma for me is what distance to run. I contemplate bailing at one mile, 3000 km, 20 minutes, and various other checkpoints I create along the way. At each of these checkpoints, a decision needs to be made, and when I remain undecided I feel that the gradient of the treadmill is increased and the activity starts to become that much harder. When I decide and commit ahead of time that I am running three miles that day, the process becomes more enjoyable, and once I am into my stride, the experience becomes that much more fluid and powerful.

Indecision weighs heavy, and the more time you spend considering the plethora of possibilities the more friction you apply to your potential being realized. Success breeds success, and indecision is the biggest enemy to you adding victories to your life.

Progress onward from achieving success with your first checkpoint is dependent on your ability to move forward quickly. Moving quickly results in your adding together much of what you have learned in this book so far and being able to answer one very impactful and complex question over and over again. The question could be phrased as ...

- "Now what?"
- "What now?"
- "What happens next?"
- "What is the next step?"
- "What do I do now?"

If you know my work, you will be aware of my fascination with words and their impact on our behaviors. The words in these questions are important for some very specific and powerful reasons. In each case, the framing of the question has all of the vital ingredients to promote progress:

- They are future-focused.
- They imply personal responsibility.
- They evoke decisive actions.

Answering these questions is harder than it sounds, and you can take five bold actions to make answering them easier and easier:

1. **Do more of what you do**. As a professional speaker, the best thing I can do to assist my decision-making process is to speak more. I know that the more I work material, the more I can grow in confidence with that material, and every time I find myself at a crossroads, the experience of my activity serves me. I speak on stage, on podcasts, in interviews, at family events, and even stand-up comedy venues, and every time I speak, the experience added is valuable to me. Speakers speak, writers write, bakers bake, and leaders lead. Whatever your BIG idea is, spend more time in activities related to where you want to move toward.

2. **Mix in the right circles**. The company you keep provides a rich resource of evidence to support your own decision-making process. Observing how others behave in your space provides you role models to consider and second-hand experience to reference. Invest seriously in committing time to be in and around those you wish to emulate and learn from.

3. **Seek targeted feedback**. One thing everyone loves to give is an opinion, and when you requested opinions from the right people, their insight can be remarkably valuable. Be careful when asking for advice from others that you present your questions in a proactive and decisive way:

- Instead of asking "What do you think I should do?," ask "What would you do if you were in my shoes?"

- Instead of asking "Did you like it?," "What did you think?," or "How did I do?," ask "What three things did you like best?" and "If you could improve just one thing, where would you focus?"

- Instead of asking "How much should I charge?," ask "What have you seen others with my experience charge?"

If you ask in a more deliberate and constructive way, the advice you receive can be more practical, applicable, and often more honest.

4. **Plan little victories.** In many careers the milestones that support your personal growth are mapped with promotion milestones, bonuses, incentives, and more. When managing yourself, these initiatives can be just as effective; it's just that you are responsible for defining the checkpoints and the rewards. By creating a number of predetermined if/then scenarios, you can use incentives you created to drive your actions. "If I achieve X, then I will reward myself with Y."

5. **Define your review process.** Procrastination is created by your internal inability to process your situation. By defining the process you will use for self-appraisal ahead of time, you can speed up your own efficiency in moving forward. My review process following every major event has become very simple and can vary in its intensity following different activities, but the process is always the same. I ask myself two questions, in the same order, and always

exhaust the answers to question 1 before moving to question 2:

Question 1: What went well?
Question 2: What would I do differently next time?

Documenting the answers to these questions helps anchor my experience and provide valuable reference points to support all future decisions.

As you progress, there will be obstacles, diversions, and distractions and—just like a river—your work is never done. Also, just like a river, once it has momentum, consistency, and power, it can be used to fuel so much, carry so many, and move through countless barriers. Momentum is your friend, and although your ultimate success can be influenced by many miracles outside of your control, you can create much luck for yourself on the journey.

Win when you are winning and ride the waves when they appear. Be prepared that sometimes you will be making decisions in the moment that are unplanned, off course, but still the right thing to do.

Develop simple criteria like the question: "What better options do I currently have to move me closer to my goal?" If the answer is "none," then ride the wave and see where it takes you. This very mindset has resulted in the organic harvesting of hundreds of my personal achievements, not because I designed them perfectly, but because I had something to run toward. The decisions on the way presented me with options to travel paths that were better than the ones I was traveling at that moment, and I rode the wave, made bold choices, and above all else, kept moving forward.

Your Action Step
Plan Your Victories

With so much to think about to fuel your journey, I am sure you have already crafted a number of personal actions that require your attention. One that can be easily missed and could be the critical ingredient in your ability to go the distance is your ability to plan your personal reward checkpoints.

Earlier in the chapter we talked about creating conditional outcomes by using if/then to build your own incentive plan. For your action step, I want you to share my belief in you and remove all the conditions; instead turn your possibilities into absolutes and define your progress prizes.

This means that your activity is to write between three and nine nonnegotiable incentive statements that point back to your personal efforts and show gratitude toward your achievements. Your sentences move from conditional to nonnegotiable simply by swapping the word "if" for the word "when."

"When X happens, then my reward will be Y."

Document your statements, keep them visible in your world, and—for added accountability—share them with your loved ones.

PHIL**osophys** ─────────

"Your success is in direct correlation to your ability to make smart, timely, and purposeful decisions."

@philmjonesuk

─────────

9
Upgrade Your Operating System

Making something happen for yourself means that the one person you are likely to spend more time in conversation with than anybody else is YOU. Often overlooked is the impact this internal dialogue has on your beliefs, actions, and outcomes. You are reading this book because you want to make a change, and resisting that change are not only your existing network and environment, but also the internal voice that you have spent your life training, which can often be confusing, demotivating, and self-sabotaging. One of a few components you are in full control of through this experience is how you *choose* to think, and if we define "thinking" as nothing more than "the conversations you have that nobody else hears and that matter the most," you will quickly realize why giving this some attention is paramount.

I said a second ago that your internal voice has been trained through your history, so to help you work through achieving your BIG idea your existing thought process may need to reconditioned and a few upgrades added if it is to support you properly on your journey.

Choose your voice. A challenge I fight with every day is that for over 20 years I have worked for one of the most demanding, relentless, and unforgiving bosses on the planet. The person I am describing is me and, albeit one of the factors that fuels my ambition, I have had to learn to filter the way in which I hear this internal voice. When my voice is being mean, I hear it in the voice of someone I don't respect (Remember the dreamer story from Chapter 2?), and when it's being supportive and uplifting, I hear the voice of my amazing grandmother, Nan. Simply applying these voices to my internal dialogue changes how I listen to what is being said, and the result is a more constructive conversation. More than just choosing how the voices sound, I have briefed them on the qualities I am looking for that support me and my insecurities. Knowing how I work, I look for the undertone of all my internal conversations to be conducted with three powerful values that my conscious mind can check back with:

- Kind
- Fair
- Purposeful

These three criteria ensure that almost every internal conversation protects my ego (kind), is built from a position of honesty (fair), and is action-focused (purposeful).

Keep one foot in the future. Going through change is rarely without challenge, but it is worth it in the long run if your reason is big enough to work for. Clarity on the visions you have for your future life is essential, and the more vivid your dreams about the idea that fuels your ambition, then the more likely you are to work through tough times. These can be written goals, dream boards, aspirational artifacts, or whatever works for you. The key here is that, in tough times, your mind jumps to your purpose and not to the problem you are facing.

Hypothetical mentors. My self-dialogue can often involve other voices that I choose to chat with based on my hypothetical knowledge of their belief systems. I often ask myself: "What would [insert person] do/think/say?" Having chosen my squad of mentors and their roles, I get the benefit of their wisdom.

Control the conversation. Labeling something as right or wrong can have devastating consequences to your progress. Questions often asked of me by audiences in my training events start with: "What is the best way to…?" Striving for the "best" way is hugely counterproductive to your success and promotes limiting self-beliefs. If you are aiming at your "best," you have decided that there is an absolute destination where "best" is realized. Experience has taught me that there is unlikely to be a "best" way to do anything or a "best" outcome, nor did anyone ever truly try his or her "best." Instead, if we shift our internal thought processes to becoming relentlessly "better," we create a never-ending journey of improvement. Innovation to me is nothing more than the relentless quest for "better."

The most important question. A question that can typically cut through the noise of any self-sabotaging self-talk is: "How do I benefit from not doing this?" By looking for evidence to support the wrong side of the argument, I can often clear up any confusion and ensure that my mind stays focused on making progress toward the goal.

Despite all the work you might do to train your thought processes, you still need a manual override. This is the human equivalent of "turning it off and turning it on again." As you become more experienced in having constructive conversations with yourself, your ability to reboot can become more and more efficient.

The three main processes I use to help reboot are as follows:

- **Change of state.** Going for a run, taking a shower, cooking some food, watching a show, reading a book, or listening to music are all tools I use to reset my thought processes when I realize that my thoughts are not serving me well.

- **Phone a friend.** Your real friends are your most important emotional crutch as you work through your BIG idea. The primary job of your friends here is to listen, to understand, and to care. You are not looking for their advice, so be careful not to let them think that's what you are looking for—you have mentors, coaches, and advisors for advice!

- **Use props.** Filling your environment with powerful artifacts that bring you good energy can mean that in a single glance your thoughts are adjusted. My travel bag is full of mementos that make my heart sing; my home office is decorated with mementos of past successes, family pictures, and items that inspire me, and next to my desk is a custom print I had produced of a poem that I once wrote in tough times—if you would like to read the poem, please visit www.philmjones.com/poem.

Your Action Step

Write Your Scripts

Computer programs run on scripts or codes written to help define actions following external input. These scripts together create the entire operating system for the software or program. Take all that you have learned from this chapter and apply it by writing yourself some powerful scripts in the form of affirmations that keep you on track.

An affirmation should be written in the present tense and with the future in mind. It typically starts with the words "I am ..." and is followed with the exact circumstances that you benefit from being reminded about. Affirmations can be aspirational, purposeful, and grounding. It works best if you are courageous enough to write them down and have them visible in your space to support your thinking. Your affirmations are meant to support you and your internal dialogue, so there is no need for sharing.

Contradicting that, and for the purpose of helping you, here are some of mine:

I am strong, capable, and in control.

I am kind, caring, and often place others ahead of myself.

I am giving in nature and never give to receive.

I choose my battles and know when to walk away.

I enjoy learning new things and learn best from trying.

I am not always right, and I love to learn from others.

I am being watched and behave how I want others to see me.

I am on stage and serving an audience of millions.

These rules continue to help shape my thinking, impact my feelings, drive my actions, and create my results. You can write and rewrite yours as often as you need to.

PHILosophy ───────

"If you do not know why you are doing it, then why are you doing it?"
                    @philmjonesuk

───────

10
Control Your Controllables

Despite the fact that most people are looking outward and toward the world to define their success, it is still highly unlikely that someone is coming to save you from your existing circumstances and realize your BIG idea for you. It is likely that achieving success will require hard work, dedication, and your ability to change; however, it may not be an awful and painful journey. Perhaps the biggest realization for you to accept throughout your journey is that there is a huge amount that you are in control of and a huge amount that you have no control over at all. Our world is full of areas beyond our control and acknowledging that some-things are effected purely by chance can actually be quite liberating.

The crazy variables deliver some of the best surprises and most challenging obstacles as you navigate from one BIG idea to the next, and the areas you are in complete control of always require the most attention. Remove emotion and attention from all external factors that are outside of your control and replace them with awareness and acceptance, which allows you to pour your emotion and attention into the activities for which your efforts will have an impact on the outcomes.

Your experience, environment, competition, circumstances, and more can easily become distractions and excuses as you attempt to progress with your BIG idea. Giving too much attention to external factors continues to be one of the biggest risks in preventing your BIG idea from reaching reality.

When you find yourself making excuses, blaming others, or denying the truth, then your first thought should be "What am I going to be doing about it?"

In my life, there have been more scenarios than I can remember when external circumstances outside of my control have negatively impacted my success, and in almost every one of those circumstances I have made a decision within my control that created progress in a new direction.

If you don't have the experience, think: "How can I get the experience?"

When I started in my speaking and training business, no large clients would book me, as I had no experience, no testimonials, and no evidence of me being able to deliver. They wanted to see me delivering to satisfied audiences and share feedback with them about the results they could expect. Instead of letting this be a problem,

I hosted my own events, spoke at other people's events to sell tickets for my own programs, and built the necessary experience to gain some long-term success.

If the environment is against you, think: "How can I use the environment to my advantage?"

When I was in the retail businesses, within the world of soccer, the one thing that would affect our sales the most on match was the weather. Every time it rained, our footfall would drop by as much as 70 percent, and sales would drop also. Instead of using the weather as an excuse, we stocked up on rain jackets and umbrellas and made up for our shortfall in footfall by raising awareness of the rainwear we had available and we secured new seasonal sales instead.

If your market is saturated, think: "How can I stand out?"

In our property business, we were being challenged by lots of other companies entering the market offering similar products at similar prices, and the space was becoming very crowded. Instead of getting into price wars, we chose to differentiate by becoming a specialist in a very lucrative niche. Instead of continuing as an investment property business, we became an investment property business for dentists. This pivot allowed us to stand out in our environment and clearly differentiate from the competition.

If you cannot afford something, think: "What can I do to make this my advantage?"

In my early business, we could not afford a website or any online presence to represent us properly. Instead of complaining about it, we used it as a point of difference and shared with our clients and future clients that we worked by invitation and with hand-selected clients only. Our service was so bespoke and we were so busy we didn't advertise, and the only way you could contact us was directly by phone.

Success is desired by the many, yet only the few are prepared to apply the necessary and consistent effort. Also, when an external factor negatively impacts on the ability to succeed, it can be used to validate underperformance. In every situation when you are faced with things that you cannot affect, there is always an abundance of things that you can affect, and giving those things your energy and effort is how you step ahead of the pack.

When you study the success stories of almost every great adventurer, athlete, or entrepreneur, one recurring theme is that they always focused on the factors that were inside their control and awareness and acceptance for the factors that were not.

Contrary to popular belief, something else that you are in complete control of is the ability to give up. The advice to "Never give up" is something I believe to be entirely misinterpreted by the majority.

Persistency and determination to achieve your BIG idea are worth working for, yet achieving long-term success is likely to mean that you give up on a number of great ideas. Not every great idea will realize itself, and often it is the intelligence to let something go and start something new that allows you to evolve your own BIG idea into something that is both BIGGER and BETTER than anything you could have first imagined.

Holding onto the belief that the destination is nonnegotiable, but the journey has many routes to get you there, keeps you in control. I have without question failed with hundreds of ventures and given up instead of applying myself to something different, in a different way, to achieve something very similar. There are an infinite number of ways to achieve success in your BIG idea, with many of those ways still not invented, considered, or possible. Sometimes a change in circumstances or resources opens a new door, and sometimes it is just about timing and good fortune. Give up the plans that don't work, give up on the plans that make success harder than it needs to be, and enjoy the puzzle of continuing to work out better ways to achieve your goals.

There are, however, some things that you should never give up on:

- Never forget where you came from.
- Never forget who has helped you on the journey.
- Never forget why you are doing it.

And some things you should always do:

- Always remember to thank the people who helped you start.
- Always remember to thank the people who keep you going.
- Always remember to reward yourself with the reason you started.

Saying YES to this will have consequences— you will miss out on things, so be certain who you are doing it for because your life and their lives depend on it.

Your Action Steps

JEDI

There is a strong possibility that you may have come this far in the book and not followed the actions I've instructed you in. There is a chance you wanted to see the whole thing before you made a move any way. Your success is only going to be influenced by your actions. Great ideas are abundant, it's being one of the few who is brave enough, committed enough, and dedicated enough to follow the steps who stand a chance of bringing that idea to life.

An acronym that was bought to life in one of my coaching groups was the word JEDI.

Not only does the word refer to powerful warriors in the movie *Star Wars*, but it has a further embodiment as an evolution of the infamous Nike slogan "Just do it." I have never been one for profanities in my work, yet sometimes the suggestion of an expletive adds a little extra spice to what we are saying.

The result was that the "E" in JEDI stood for "Effing." The result was that the members in the group would decide to have JEDI moments or JEDI days. On a JEDI day it would mean they would "Just Effing Do It." This is your moment to JEDI.

Start from the beginning again and take the actions that you need to take. Do the work as you go, and I mean it, DO THE WORK. Nothing happens unless you make it happen, and following the steps I've described has created success, after success, after success.

1. Letter to self
2. Done-it list
3. Discover and document the answers to six powerful questions
4. Document your plan
5. Make a press release
6. Complete a life laundry
7. Define and realize your first checkpoint
8. Plan your victories

9. Write your scripts

10. JEDI

I promise that everything is highly unlikely to work out as planned; it is the fluidity of your movement between your actions that means you learn more at every step; those lessons lead to more movement, that movement keeps you progressing, and as long as you are moving forward, you are increasing your probabilities of making your BIG idea your reality.

PHILosophy ————

"Success is created
by doing the basics,
to a high standard,
consistently."

@philmjonesuk

A Final Thought

There is no doubt that this book could have easily been five times longer and that each chapter could have been filled with detailed research and even more information and examples. My thought is that a book like that would not help you to achieve what this book is intended to do—get you started. Too many big books decorate bookshelves and daunt their owners by never being read. I challenged myself to write the shortest BIG book I could—something full of practical information with no padding and nothing extra.

The result is that I expect you are still left with a handful of unknowns, lingering uncertainties, and some of the anxieties you had at the start of the read. The book is titled *Exactly Where to Start* for a reason. This is to nudge you into the game and help you move from idea to reality; the blanks belong to you. Your responsibility to is to start on your own journey, take the massive action required. Anything missing at this point is for you to figure out while on the journey. Don't over-think it. Just get started, keep learning, and always fail forward—your life depends on it.

One more thing: I believe in you.

Acknowledgments

Producing this book has been a very different experience from any of my earlier books. The process of creating it has been the most insular and solo effort of any piece I have produced to date.

Despite my introverted approach to its creation, a few people I know for certain have played bigger roles in its coming to life than perhaps they are even aware of.

First, there is the insanely talented and kind-hearted Scott Stratten, who found the time to speak with me and ask me the smart questions to help me realize that I was capable of producing this book within the crazy timescales required to meet the publishing deadlines.

Second, thanks to two of the most impressive people on the planet for their insanely honest and powerful contributions during the writing process. Mitch Joel, you are a wonderful friend, and your rapid-fire editorial notes within my early drafts were pure gold and have certainly helped me to raise the bar as a writer. Melissa Agnes, your continued support, ability to ask me questions that nobody else would, and encouragement to stay true to the look, feel, and style of my vision for the "Exactly" series has been a gift beyond compare.

To my incredible assistant, Bonnie. Thank you for being the single biggest reason that I manage to get so much done; thank you for always having my back; and thank you for your continued commitment to my ambition.

Then there are the people who have placed their trust in me to help them through their journeys. I couldn't possibly name all who have contributed to the knowledge and experience required to write this book, but Joy, Rachel, Kathryn, Poppy, Maria, and Rellu certainly stand out. They are all exceptional products of this very process, and their continued success, ability to be self-sufficient, and long-term friendship always inspire.

Mum and Dad, thank you for giving me the courage to start, the support to keep going, and the security of your everlasting love.

Charlotte, you rock my world, and my love for you delivers me the fuel I need to keep growing, to keep supporting others, and to show up for work every day. It's the right now that we live for and the future we are creating that provides my passion to keep bringing our BIG ideas to life.

The biggest thank you of all goes to you, and the millions just like you. Your persistent and consistent aspiration to be better, to want more, and to realize more of your ambition is what fuels me to help support those goals and knock down your barriers. I started this work because of my love of entrepreneurship, my passion for growth, and my desire to see others achieve more of what I know they are capable of achieving. All the time the world has aspirations I am thankful. Please keep finding reasons for us all to remain on the relentless quest for better.

About the Author

Phil entered the world of business at the tender age of 14. With nothing more than a bucket and sponge, he went from single-handedly washing cars on weekends to hiring a fleet of friends working on his behalf, resulting in him earning more than his teachers did by the time he was 15.

Soon after, at just 18, Phil was offered the role of sales manager with the UK's favorite department store group, making him the youngest sales manager in the company's history.

His early career went from strength to strength, as he worked with a host of Premier League football clubs to help them agree to sponsorships and licensing agreements, to then being a key part of growing a £240m property business.

But in 2008, after several years of being one of the most in-demand young business leaders in the UK, Phil decided it was time to dedicate his future to helping others to succeed. He took everything he had learned about business from his previous roles and created a training organization that delivers to people the practical skills they need to deliver the success they are looking for.

Now the author of multiple international bestselling books and the youngest winner of the coveted "British Excellence in Sales and Marketing Award," Phil is currently one of the most in-demand assets to companies worldwide.

He is by no means your typical business expert. Phil is famous for his inspiring "Magic Words" and his highly engaging, practical approach to what is often a subject that is littered with hype and power-hungry "gurus."

His vast knowledge and experience can be simplified into three areas:

1. **Acquiring** more customers

2. **Having** them come back more often

3. **Helping** them spend more when they shop

With experience training more than two million people globally and having delivered more than 2,000 presentations in over 50 countries across five continents, Phil has a busy and active travel schedule. He defines his passion as helping others to realize more of their potential.

When not on the road, you will find him at home in New York City or in his peaceful retreat in Buckinghamshire, England.

A Shameless Plug

Hi there,

I created this book to be a quick and simple tool to help you to make the start that you need in turning your BIG idea into reality. It's all about delivering you a blueprint to get started and to guide you through the steps required, holding your hand, and delivering you a path to follow.

If you enjoyed the book and took value from it, then there are some simple steps you can take to show your gratitude to the author. A few of these things are listed below, and if you feel compelled to do so, then I would be most grateful of your support:

- Take a moment to leave a positive review on amazon.com.
- Share a photo of you and the book on social media at #exactlywheretostart.

- Introduce the book to others in your world and tell them about its impact.
- Buy a copy as a gift for someone else.
- Include an editorial review on your website or blog.
- Send me a note on social media with your top takeaways.

These small actions really make all the difference to us authors and could play a major part in helping someone else to turn his or her BIG idea into something real.

Thanks a million,

www.philmjones.com

Index